Gingerbread Houses For Kids

by Jennifer A. Ericsson

illustrated by Beth L. Blair

D1205259

White Birch Press

P. O. Box 1433 ★ Concord ★ New Hampshire ★ 03302-1433

GINGERBREAD HOUSES FOR KIDS
By Jennifer A. Ericsson
Illustrated by Beth L. Blair

Published by White Birch Press
P.O. Box 1433
Concord, NH   03302-1433

Printed in the United States of America by Wallace Press/Reprographics, Concord, NH

Publisher's Cataloging in Publication

Ericsson, Jennifer A.

Gingerbread houses for kids / by Jennifer A. Ericsson ; illustrated by Beth L. Blair.

Concord, NH : White Birch Press, c1998.

64 p. : ill. (some col.); 28 cm.

Summary: A craft book with step-by-step instructions and
patterns for six child-sized gingerbread houses.

1. Blair, Beth L.   I. Gingerbread houses.   II. Christmas cookery.
III. Holiday cookery.   IV. Holiday decorations.   V. Handicraft.

641.8654 (741.59412)   0-9661204-0-X   97-091127

ISBN 0-9661204-0-X
Library of Congress Catalog Card Number 97-091127

10 9 8 7 6 5 4 3 2 1
First Edition

This book is dedicated to Jan Murray
and all the Gingerbread Villagers who have
taught me everything I know.

JAE

To mommo and dad, who taught me
to draw with a sense of humor;
To Christopher, who brings me lovely cups of tea;
and to Jennifer – what fun (when I'm not hysterical)!

BLB

Many people offered assistance in the making of this book.
I heartily give thanks to:

The members of St. George's Episcopal Church in Middlebury, CT for sharing the gingerbread and icing recipes they have developed over 25 years of building their annual Gingerbread Village.

My father, William A. Barber, for his example and support.

My daughter, Annie, and her friends, Gretchen Andrus, Jennifer Bueddeman, Laura Fries, and Emilie Rider, who spent a beautiful summer weekend indoors testing the manuscript and building all the houses.

The following people for their helpful comments and suggestions for improvement: Janet Banks–Mott, William A. Barber, Christopher Blair, Charlotte Buxton, Paul Ericsson, Elizabeth Foy, Charlotte Janis, Kathy Kiernan, Margaret Lannamann, Fran McGlynn, Jan Murray, Lori Nerbonne, Margy Rider, Joyce Tarpey, and Suzie Woods.

My husband, Paul, for having Faith.

My best friend and illustrator, Beth, for helping to make this book a reality. I couldn't have done it without her!

JAE

Table Of Contents

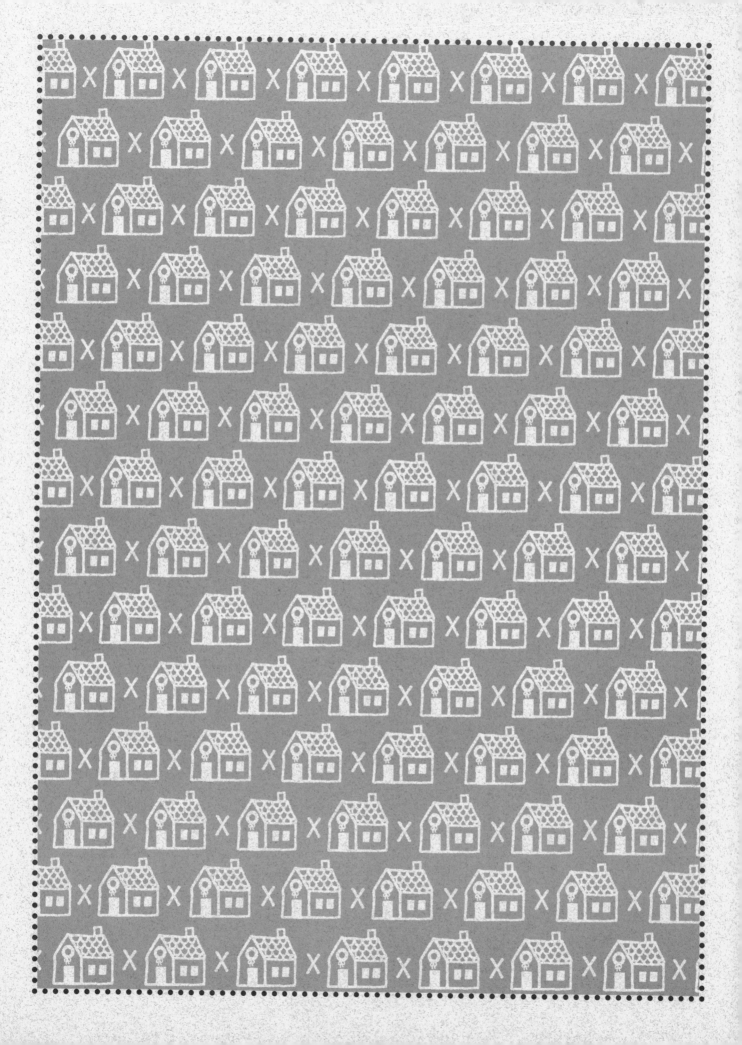

Introduction

I love building gingerbread houses! I fell in love the first time I wandered into St. George's Episcopal Church in Middlebury, CT, fifteen years ago. The parishioners were preparing their annual Gingerbread Village, and I asked if I could watch. Jan Murray sat me down, set me up with four walls for a very tiny cottage and told me, "The only way to learn is to do." I've been doing ever since – and loving every minute!

Over the years, I realized there was a need for a book introducing children to this craft. Also, many adults I knew were intimidated by the glossy houses shown on the covers of women's magazines each fall. They thought it might be fun to try building a house, but wanted smaller, simpler projects. Ideas swirled for such a book, and *Gingerbread Houses For Kids* was born.

One of the fun challenges of making gingerbread houses is constructing them using only edible items. There is no mention of glue, cardboard, or shellac in this book. I feel very strongly that if something <u>looks</u> good enough to eat, you should be able to eat it!

Like any other craft, building gingerbread houses requires certain equipment and skills. But the equipment is not terribly expensive nor the skills difficult to learn. With a little time, patience, and imagination, you can discover the gingerbread artist within yourself. And maybe, just maybe, you'll fall in love – just like I did.

Part I: The Basics

"Do you know the Grimm's fairy tale, <u>Hansel and Gretel</u>? Since being published in the 1800's, it has inspired many people to build gingerbread houses. If you've never read this story, check it out at your local library!"

Step 1: The Pattern

The first thing you need to make a gingerbread house is a pattern. We will start by using the pattern for the Cottage, the most basic project in the book. Once you have followed the step-by-step instructions for this simple house, you will have the skills necessary to build any of the others. The patterns for the Chalet, Church, Barn, School, and Castle are located in Part II of this book, along with their special building instructions.

To make a pattern:

1. All of the patterns are shown actual size, but <u>DO NOT CUT THEM OUT OF THE BOOK!</u> Photocopy the patterns you want to use. For this first project, photocopy the Cottage pattern found on these two pages.

2. With scissors, cut out the pattern pieces from the photocopy.

3. Cut out the windows by carefully poking a hole in the center of the window and snipping toward the edge. Cut out the door, too.

"Try your best to cut nice, straight edges."

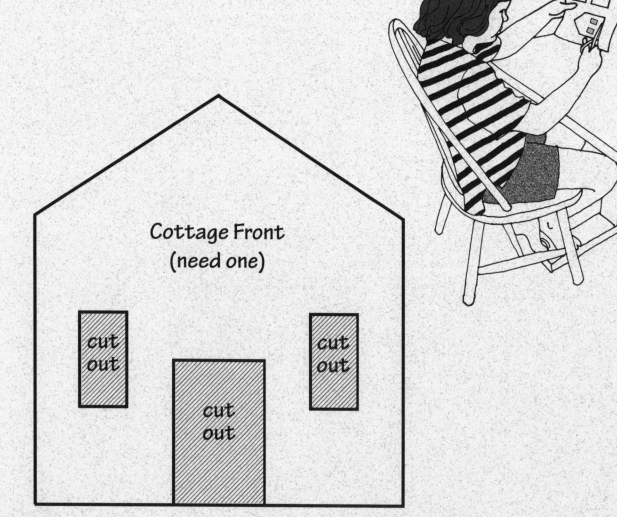

Cottage Front
(need one)

cut out

cut out

cut out

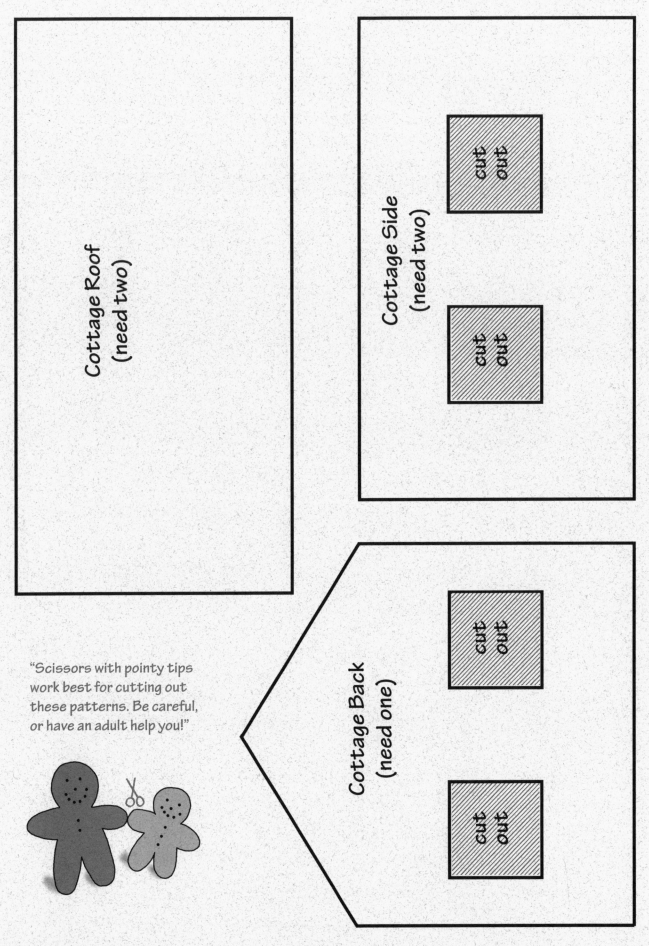

Cottage Roof
(need two)

Cottage Side
(need two)

cut out

cut out

Cottage Back
(need one)

cut out

cut out

"Scissors with pointy tips work best for cutting out these patterns. Be careful, or have an adult help you!"

Step 2: The Dough

Gingerbread dough is the basic ingredient in your house.
It is easy to handle – and tastes great!

To make the dough, you will need the following equipment:

* stove

* large pot (8 quart)

* wooden spoon

* measuring cup (1 cup)

* 2 measuring spoons (1 teaspoon, 1 tablespoon)

* mixing bowl (medium-sized)

* large cutting board

* plastic wrap

One batch of dough should be more than enough to make any one house, <u>except</u> for the Castle (which will take two batches). You can make cookies with the extra dough or save it in case any of the pieces break.

Gingerbread Dough ingredients:

* 1 cup butter or margarine (2 sticks)

* 1 cup sugar

* 1 cup unsulphured molasses

* 5 cups flour

* 1 teaspoon baking soda

* 1 teaspoon nutmeg

* 1 teaspoon salt

* 1 tablespoon ginger

SUCCESS TIP:
Make sure you have everything you need <u>before</u> you get started.

"ONLY use a stove
with an adult's help!"

1. Over low heat, melt the butter in the large pot. When it is melted, keep the pot on the burner, but turn off the heat. Stir in the sugar and molasses.

2. In the mixing bowl, mix together 1 cup of flour and the baking soda, nutmeg, salt, and ginger. Add to the wet ingredients in the pot. Mix well. Stir in 3 more cups of flour.

3. Sprinkle half of the last cup of flour onto the cutting board. Scoop the dough out of the pot onto the flour. Sprinkle the rest of the flour over the sticky lump of dough. Knead the flour into the dough.

4. The finished dough should be smooth and easy to handle. If the dough is still sticky, knead in more flour, 1/4 cup at a time, until it feels smooth.

5. Wrap the dough in plastic wrap to keep it soft. Dough will stay fresh for several days if you refrigerate it. Be sure to bring it to room temperature and reknead it before using. Dough can also be frozen.

How To Knead

Fold dough from the sides into the middle and push fold with the heel of your hand. Repeat until all flour is worked into the dough. Turn or flip dough as necessary.

Fold dough
into middle.

Push fold in
with heel of hand.

Step 3: Rolling & Cutting

The dough is made. Now you need to roll it out on cookie sheets and trace the house pattern onto it.

You will need the following equipment:

* damp dish towel (or paper towel)
* 2-3 cookie sheets (the type with one or two raised edges preferred)
* rolling pin
* plastic wrap
* small sharp knife
* gingerbread house pattern
* no-stick cooking spray

1. Lay a wet towel on a table or countertop. Place a cookie sheet on top of it. The wet towel keeps the cookie sheet from moving while you're rolling out the dough.

2. Take a handful of dough about the size of a baseball or orange. Place it on an ungreased cookie sheet and cover it the long way with a large piece of plastic wrap. This keeps the dough from sticking to the rolling pin as you roll it out.

3. Roll out the gingerbread dough. It should be about 1/8-inch thick. Try to roll it all the same thickness and cover as much of the cookie sheet as you can. It is especially important not to have thick roof pieces. Thinner is better.

★ SUCCESS TIPS:

Run your hand over the dough. You can feel when one part is thicker than another.

It is tough to roll out the dough on a cookie sheet with four raised edges. If you can't find a cookie sheet with only 1 or 2 raised edges, flip the cookie sheet you do have over and roll out the dough on the <u>back</u>.

4. Remove the plastic wrap when you are finished rolling.

5. Lightly spray the back of the pattern pieces with no stick cooking spray. If too much spray gets on a piece, wipe it off with a paper towel.

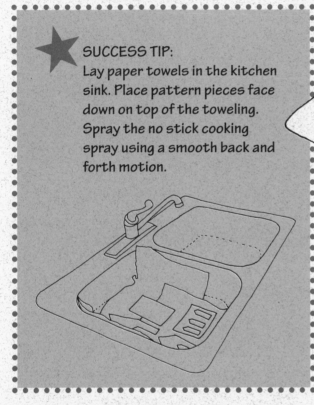

SUCCESS TIP:
Lay paper towels in the kitchen sink. Place pattern pieces face down on top of the toweling. Spray the no stick cooking spray using a smooth back and forth motion.

"ALWAYS use a knife with adult supervision!"

pieces can touch, but not overlap

cookie sheet with one raised edge

Cottage

Cottage

Cottage Roof (cut two)

small, sharp knife

1/2 inch "frame" of dough around pattern pieces

6. Place the pieces of your pattern on top of the dough. Try to fit several pieces of your house on one sheet. It's okay if the pieces touch each other, but they should not overlap.

7. With a small sharp knife, cut around the pattern. Cut the outlines for the windows and doors, but do not take them out. Carefully remove the pattern pieces from the dough by lifting under the paper with the tip of the knife.

8. Leave a 1/2-inch border all around the pieces you have traced. This frame reduces the amount of spreading that will occur when the gingerbread is baked.

Step 4: Baking & Cooling

After the pieces of the house are cut into the dough, the next step is to bake them. Because the oven, cookie sheets, and gingerbread are all REALLY HOT during this step, an adult should do this part.

You will need the following equipment:

* preheated oven (350° Fahrenheit)

* oven mitts

* cooling racks

* small sharp knife

* pancake turner

"The stove and gingerbread are HOT! Adults only, please!"

Did you know that George Washington's mother, Mary Ball Washington, supposedly made one of the best gingerbread cakes? It was very moist and would NOT have been good for gingerbread houses.

1. Put the cookie sheet(s) in the preheated oven. Bake the pieces at 350 degrees for 10 to 12 minutes. The gingerbread should turn a golden brown.

2. Remove the cookie sheets from the oven with oven mitts. If you're not sure if the gingerbread is done, touch it lightly with one of your fingers. Your touch should not leave an imprint.

SUCCESS TIP:
Use the middle rack in the oven.

<u>The next three steps must be done quickly since the pieces harden and stick as they cool!</u>

3. Immediately recut the outer edges of each piece. Gingerbread spreads as it is baked and you want really straight edges. Do not recut the windows and doors. You only need the outline on the gingerbread to guide you when you're decorating the house.

4. Cut away the gingerbread "frame" from around the pieces of the house. These tasty scraps are for eating!

5. Slide a pancake turner under each piece to keep it from sticking to the cookie sheet. Pieces can be moved to the cooling racks as soon as they will hold their shape.

COOL THE GINGERBREAD COMPLETELY BEFORE TRYING TO BUILD YOUR HOUSE!

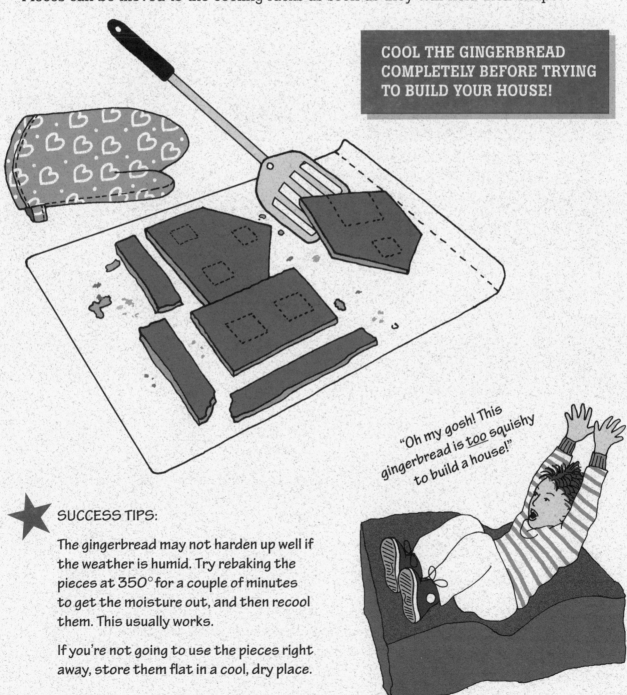

"Oh my gosh! This gingerbread is <u>too</u> squishy to build a house!"

★ SUCCESS TIPS:

The gingerbread may not harden up well if the weather is humid. Try rebaking the pieces at 350° for a couple of minutes to get the moisture out, and then recool them. This usually works.

If you're not going to use the pieces right away, store them flat in a cool, dry place.

Step 5: Checking The Edges

After the gingerbread pieces are COMPLETELY cool and hard, check the edges to make sure they are straight. This is important so that the pieces of your house fit together snugly.

Hold the front and back pieces of your house with their flat sides together. Is one piece a lot bigger than the other? Are the angles for the roof the same? If not, you need to file them so they are.

To make straight edges, you will need the following:

* gingerbread pieces

* edge of table

* wastebasket

* file

1. Lay the gingerbread pieces together on a table and stick the edge to be filed slightly over the edge of the table. Place a wastebasket underneath to catch the gingerbread dust.

2. File carefully until the edge is straight.

3. Turn the pieces and file each edge the same way. Blow off extra dust.

4. Repeat the same steps with the side and roof pieces of your house.

The ever-present cookie tin full of gingerbread scraps. Yum!

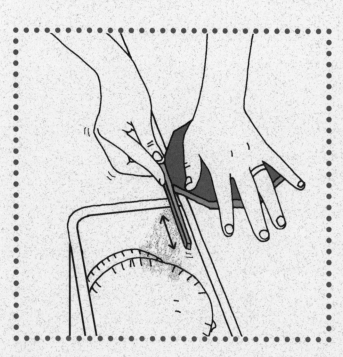

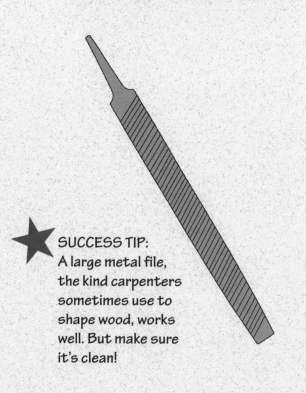

SUCCESS TIP:
A large metal file, the kind carpenters sometimes use to shape wood, works well. But make sure it's clean!

18

Step 6: Preparing A Base

You will want a flat surface on which to build your house. A base lets you move the house without touching it. Not only can you carry it out of harm's way, but you can turn the house while decorating it to easily reach all sides.

To make a base, you will need:

* a heavy piece of cardboard that doesn't bend (approximately 12 x 12 inches – larger for the Castle)

* plastic wrap

* tape

Cover the cardboard with the plastic wrap. Tape ends underneath.

The base is meant as a work space. After your house is done, you will either remove the plastic and decorate the cardboard as a yard, or arrange the house on another base, such as a platter.

"Did you know that ginger, the spice used in gingerbread, dates back to ancient times? It comes from the root of the ginger plant."

Step 7: The Icing

Icing is the glue that holds the pieces of your house together. It is also used for decorating.

The amount of icing required to complete each house depends on how you decide to decorate it, the number of colors you make, and how big a yard you have. Two batches should do it for all the houses EXCEPT for the Castle. That one may need three. Keep an extra box of sugar on hand, just in case.

To make the icing, you will need the following equipment:

* electric mixer
  (stand-up mixer works best)

* small mixing bowl for mixer

* measuring spoons
  (1 tablespoon, 1/4 teaspoon)

* liquid measuring cup

* rubber spatula

* plastic wrap

Meringue Icing ingredients:

* 1 box confectioners sugar, unsifted

* 3 tablespoons meringue powder

* 1/4 teaspoon cream of tartar

* 1/3 cup warm water

1. Place all ingredients in the small mixing bowl. Beat on a low speed until dry ingredients are wet. Do NOT start the mixer on a high speed or you will have sugar and meringue powder everywhere!

2. Beat on a high speed for about three minutes or until icing is stiff.

3. Cover the icing with plastic wrap when not in use.

"ONLY use an electric mixer with an adult's help!"

Meringue powder can be bought in many grocery stores or party supply stores – look in the section where cake decorating supplies are sold. It is also available in some department stores with the kitchenware.

Step 8: The Pastry Bag

To apply icing to the gingerbread pieces, you will need the following:

* 1 pastry bag
* 1 coupler
* 1 metal decorating tip (#10)
* 1 batch of icing

What Is A Pastry Bag?

A pastry bag is a cone-shaped bag with openings at both ends. They can be plastic or cloth and come in different sizes. The 8-10 inch size works well for children. Some pastry bags are reusable if you clean them after each use. Others can be thrown away after you use them.

"Pastry bags also make perfect anteater noses!"

What Is A Coupler?

Couplers are small, plastic two-pieced gadgets. One piece is the nozzle and the other is the ring. The nozzle slides inside the pastry bag and sticks out the bottom. A metal decorating tip is placed over the end of the nozzle. Then the plastic ring screws tightly over both of them. The coupler makes it easy to change decorating tips on your pastry bag.

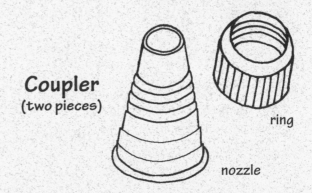

Coupler
(two pieces)

ring

nozzle

What Are Decorating Tips?

Decorating tips are small metal cones which are used on the end of a pastry bag. They come with different shapes cut out on the end. Each tip has a number – the bigger the number, the bigger the shape.

For example, here are some different sized round tips (see diagram, right):

The first tip you will use is the #10 round tip – the one with the biggest hole.

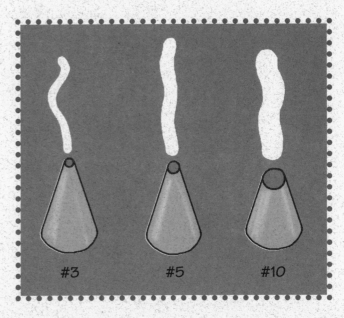

#3   #5   #10

Filling The Pastry Bag

1. Open the bag. Slide the nozzle of the coupler into the bag. If you have a new bag, you will need to cut off the end so that the nozzle can poke through.

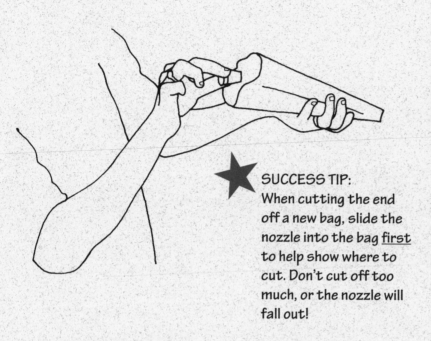

⭐ **SUCCESS TIP:**
When cutting the end off a new bag, slide the nozzle into the bag <u>first</u> to help show where to cut. Don't cut off too much, or the nozzle will fall out!

The nozzle in the pastry bag should just stick out up to the first thread.

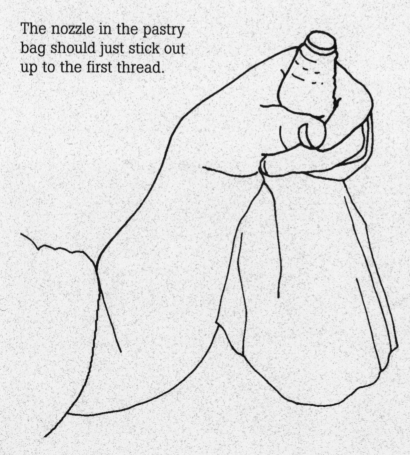

2. Place the decorating tip over the end of the nozzle.

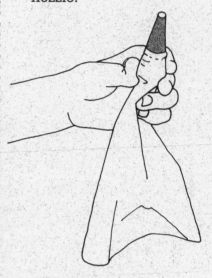

3. Put the coupler "ring" over the tip and screw tightly into place.

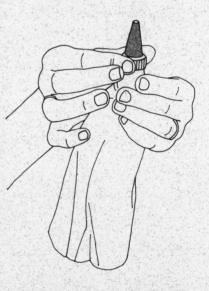

DON'T PANIC!
Filling the pastry bag is <u>very</u> easy. It just takes a lot of pictures to show all of the steps.

4. Turn the pastry bag over so the nozzle points towards the floor. Fold down the top of the pastry bag to make a 1 1/2 inch cuff – like rolling down the top of a pair of socks.

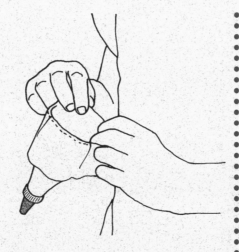

5. Using the spatula, fill the bag with icing. This is easy if the child holds the bag under the cuff and the adult scoops in the icing. Don't worry if some gets on the cuff. It will be on the inside when you're done.

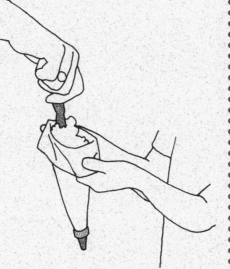

6. Turn up the cuff. Hold the top of the bag with one hand. Using the fingers of the other hand, slide the icing in the bag towards the tip at the bottom.

7. When all the icing is at the bottom of the bag, fold the top of the bag like this: Lay the bag flat on a counter or table with the tip pointing towards you. Fold the two top corners to the middle, making a triangle.

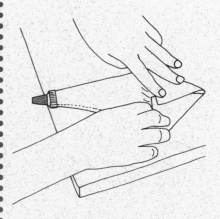

8. Roll the bag towards the decorating tip. Hold the rolled top firmly. If you don't, the icing will come out the top of the bag instead of the bottom when you squeeze!

Step 9: Putting The Pieces Together

1. Put the cardboard base in front of you. Lay the four walls of your house on top of the base. You want the flat side (the side that was against the cookie sheet) facing up. It should look like a gust of wind blew into the center of the house and made all the walls fall away from each other. Have the peak of the front of the house pointing towards your chest.

2. Using the pastry bag with the #10 tip, squeeze a large line of icing from top to bottom down both side edges of the back of the house.

3. Pick up the back piece and one side. Press together at right angles. Hold for a minute or so. They should then stay up on their own.

4. Pick up the other side piece and press into the second line of icing. You should have two right angles.

5. Squeeze two lines of icing down the side edges of the front of the house.

6. Pick up the front of the house and press it against the sides already assembled. You want the pieces to fit snugly together. Don't be afraid to move them or apply more icing.

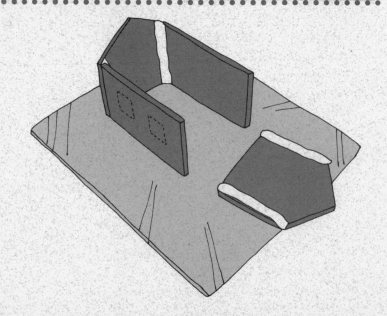

7. To reinforce the house, squeeze a large line of icing up each inside corner.

8. Run your finger up the icing. This pushes it into any cracks.

9. DO NOT ATTACH THE ROOF! The roof goes on last – <u>after</u> the sides are decorated.

10. Let your house harden well before decorating it. Let it stand at least 30 minutes – or even better, overnight. If you try to decorate it before it has hardened, it may come apart!

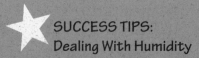

SUCCESS TIPS: Dealing With Humidity

Humidity makes the gingerbread soft and can cause your house to collapse. This is especially true if you plan to decorate it with heavy candy.

You can ice the inside of your house to guard against humidity. This is easier to do BEFORE you assemble the walls. Be sure to run your finger along the edge of each piece to get rid of any lumps or blobs of icing that stick out and would keep the pieces from fitting together smoothly. Let the icing dry before putting the walls together.

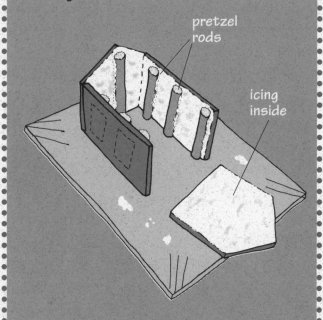

pretzel rods

icing inside

Pretzel rods or bread sticks also can be used to reinforce your house. Use pieces that will fit up and down on the INSIDE of the house without going higher than the house edges. Use icing to attach them in place. One rod up the middle of each piece and a couple on the sides should add enough support.

Step 10: Decorating Plan

There is no <u>right</u> way to decorate a gingerbread house. Two houses built from the same pattern can look totally different depending on how they are decorated. Your choices are limited only by your imagination! But...before you rush into it...

STOP AND THINK! What do you want your house to look like when it's done?

A decorating plan is a good thing to have. Browse through the rest of the book to get ideas for walls, windows, doors, roofs, and yards. What colors of icing will you make? What decorating tips will you try? What candies, nuts, or cereals do you like?

Make decisions and write down EVERYTHING you will need to decorate your house. Remember that many useful items may already be in your kitchen cabinets.

For each part of your house, list the style, the colors of icing you will need, and which decorating tips you will use. Be sure to also note the candies, cookies, or other food items you will need to decorate your house and yard.

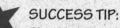

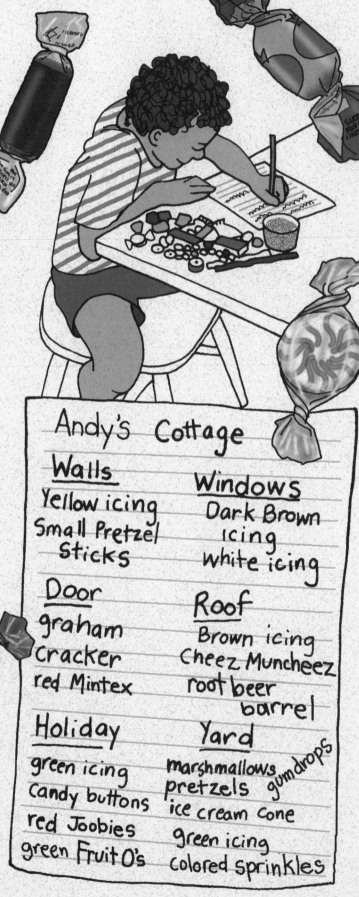

Andy's Cottage

Walls
Yellow icing
Small Pretzel Sticks

Windows
Dark Brown icing
white icing

Door
graham Cracker
red Mintex

Roof
Brown icing
Cheez Muncheez
root beer barrel

Holiday
green icing
Candy buttons
red Joobies
green Fruit O's

Yard
marshmallows gumdrops
pretzels
ice cream Cone
green icing
colored sprinkles

★ SUCCESS TIP:
Check to be sure you have <u>all</u> the ingredients you need BEFORE you get started. Once you put the icing on the house, you won't have time to run to the store!

Step 11: Coloring The Icing

The recipe in this book makes WHITE icing. Adding food coloring allows you to make other colors. Paste food coloring works much better than the liquid drops. The liquid drops dilute the icing and it's hard to make bright colors with it. You can get food coloring paste at stores that sell cake decorating supplies. It comes in small jars and lasts a long time.

To color icing, you will need:

* icing (recipe page 20)
* food coloring paste(s)
* toothpicks
* spoon(s)
* small airtight containers (such as margarine tubs or yogurt containers)
* corn syrup

1. Make a batch of icing. Divide it into containers. How many will depend on the number of colors you need (check your decorating plan).

2. Using a toothpick, add a small amount of paste(s) to the icing. BE CAREFUL – THE COLORS STAIN! Mix well with a spoon.

   Here are directions for mixing some of the most popular colors:

   PURPLE .... Equal amounts RED & BLUE

   ORANGE .... Equal amounts RED & YELLOW

   PINK.............. Small dab RED

   GREEN.......... Equal amounts BLUE & YELLOW

   BROWN .... Equal amounts RED & GREEN

   GRAY............ Small dab BLACK

3. Continue to add small amounts of paste until you like the color. Keep in mind that colors darken as they dry. Also keep in mind that the lighter colors taste better since they use much less food coloring.

4. Keep icing in airtight containers until needed. If the icing should harden, add a small amount of corn syrup and mix until smooth.

During the 14th century, there were special baking "guilds" for gingerbread artists. They made grand creations decorated with icing and cloves – and sometimes with real gold. When they were finished, these structures could weigh over 100 pounds!

Step 12: The Decorating Tips

There are four shapes of decorating tips used in this book.

Round

These tips have circular openings. They are used to make dots, lines, loops, and lettering. Suggested sizes: #3, #5, and #10.

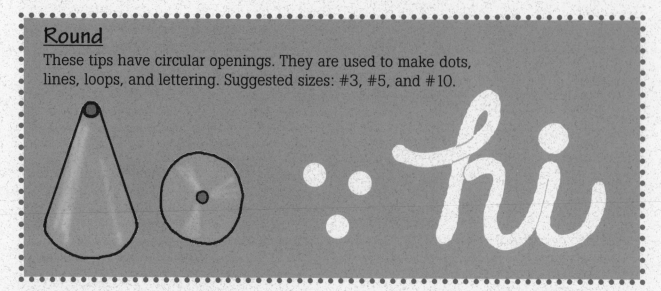

Star

These tips have star-shaped openings. They are used to make stars and ribbed borders. Suggested sizes: #14 and #18.

If you twist the tip as you pull up from making a star, you get a rosette!

Leaf

This tip has a V-shaped opening. As the name of this tip suggests, it is used for making simple leaves! Suggested size: #349 or #65.

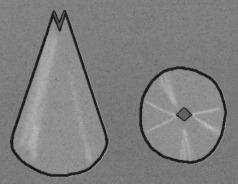

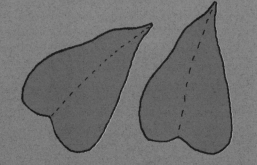

These small leaves can be used to make holly, wreaths, or other holiday decorations.

Shutter or Ribbon

This tip has a thin rectangular opening. One side is ribbed, the other is not. It is used to make shutters as well as the "clapboards" on the sides of a house. Suggested size: #47.

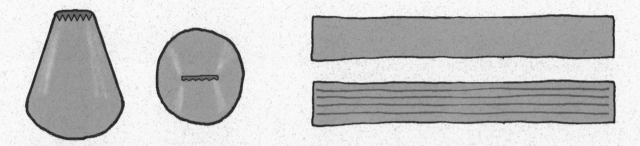

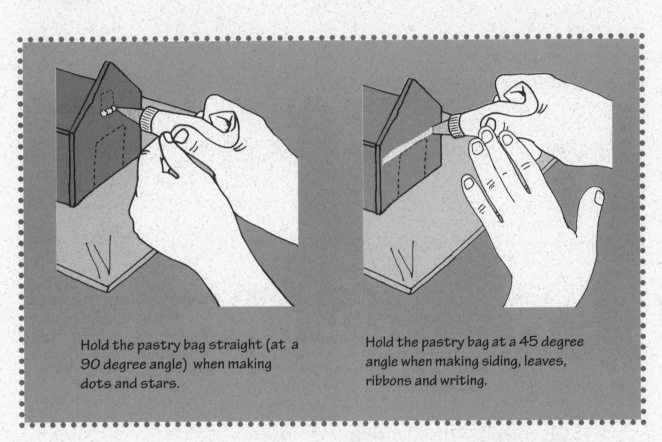

Hold the pastry bag straight (at a 90 degree angle) when making dots and stars.

Hold the pastry bag at a 45 degree angle when making siding, leaves, ribbons and writing.

 SUCCESS TIP: Practice with each tip on a piece of wax paper or a scrap of gingerbread. See what each can do! Don't be afraid to combine different shapes.

Ribbed border with stars and dots.

Ribbed shutter with dots.

Step 13: Decorating The Walls

You will decorate the walls of your house first. The look of the walls changes by putting icing on in different ways.

Smooth Walls

Using a knife, apply a smooth layer of icing to the walls. Go around the window and door outlines. A bent-handled knife makes it easier to apply frosting.

Brick Walls

Use small pieces of gum or licorice sticks as bricks. Spread icing onto a small area of the wall. Push pieces into icing.

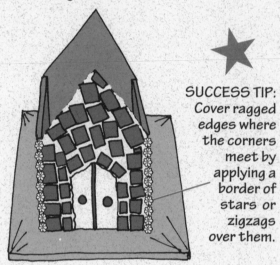

Walls With Siding

Apply a smooth layer of icing to the wall. Using a pastry bag with a small round tip, pipe lines across, or up and down, each side (use same or contrasting color).

        OR

Using a pastry bag with a shutter tip, pipe siding across, or up and down, each wall (use ribbed or flat side of tip).

        OR

Apply a smooth layer of icing to the wall. Drag a zigzag cake decorating tool through the icing. Scrape away any icing that covers the windows or door.

SUCCESS TIP: Cover ragged edges where the corners meet by applying a border of stars or zigzags over them.

Stone Walls

Use nuts, seeds, broken cookies or flat candies, gingerbread scraps, or peanut brittle for stones. Spread icing onto a small area of the wall. Push pieces into the icing.

Wooden Walls

Use pretzel sticks for logs. Apply a layer of frosting to a wall. Push pretzels into it, either up and down or sideways.

zigzag tool

One zigzag tool usually makes two or three sizes of siding.

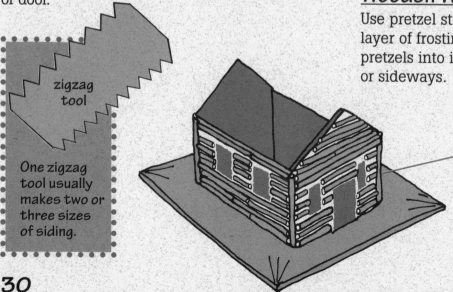

SUCCESS TIP: You can also cover ragged edges by piping a line of icing down the corners of the house and sticking on thin pretzels or candy sticks.

Step 14: Decorating The Windows

After the walls are completed, it's time to do your windows. They are applied in several steps: lighting, window panes, and shutters.

Lighting

To make it look like the lights are on in your gingerbread house, paint inside the window outlines with icing thinned with water. Suggested colors are white, yellow, orange, blue, or pink. Be sure to pick a color that goes well with the color of your walls.

You will need:

* small amount of colored icing
* paintbrush
* water

Dip the paintbrush in water and then in icing. Carefully paint inside the window outlines. The windows should look smooth and shiny. Try not to get the window color on your walls.

 SUCCESS TIPS:

Small amounts of colored icing can be mixed on a yogurt container lid or small plate. Use only enough water to smooth out the icing.

Oops! Did you frost over the outlines for your windows when decorating the walls? Many flat cookies and candies make great windows. Just attach them with icing.

Window Panes

Using a pastry bag with a small round or star tip, outline the entire window. Add lines of icing to look like window panes if desired.

no panes

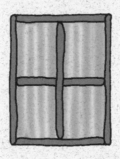 

square panes

diagonal panes

Shutters

Shutters can be made out of icing or any number of things including gum, wafer cookies, chocolate or licorice pieces, and candy canes.

To make the shutters out of icing, you will need:

* pastry bag with shutter tip

* icing of a contrasting color to your walls

1. Using either side of the shutter tip, pipe a shutter on both sides of each window.

To make the shutters with cookies, candies, or gum, you will need:

* kitchen knife

* small amount of icing

* at least two candies or cookies for EACH window on your house

1. Using the knife, spread some icing on the back of a shutter.

2. Press the shutter on one side of a window.

3. Repeat until all windows have two shutters.

icing, smooth or ribbed

small candy canes

licorice twists

striped gum with frosting stars

line of small candies

Step 15: Decorating The Door

The door may be only a small part of your house, but it's up front where everyone will notice it. Will it be plain or fancy? Do you want it to have windows or slats? What kind of doorknob would you like? Below are some suggestions for different types of doors.

Gingerbread Door

Using a pastry bag with a small round tip or small star tip, outline the entire door. Outline small windows if you like. Don't forget the doorknob!

Frosted Door

Using a pastry bag with a shutter tip, pipe door slats onto the door. Use a color that contrasts with the walls – perhaps the same color as your shutters or roof. Add a doorknob.

Cookie, Chocolate, or Gum Door

Rectangular cookies, thin sticks of gum, or small chocolate bars make delicious doors! With a knife, apply icing to the back of the cookie, chocolate, or gum. Press against the house. Add a doorknob.

Pretzel Door

With a knife, apply a layer of icing to the door. Press pretzel sticks into icing. Add a doorknob.

plain

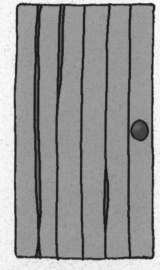

shutter tip

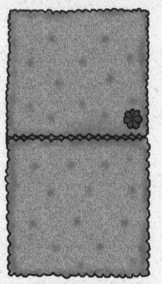

sugar cookies

pretzels with icing

chocolate with star edge

Doorknobs can be made from a dot or star of icing, or by attaching a small nut, candy, or bean.

33

Step 16: Attaching The Roof

To attach your roof you will need:

* stiff white icing

* pastry tube with a large round tip (#10)

* gingerbread roof pieces

1. Position the house so you're looking at one of the sides. Pipe a generous amount of icing down the two peak edges and across the top edge of the side of the house closest to you (see dotted brown lines, below).

2. Press one roof piece into the icing. Be sure that it is lined up evenly with the peak.

3. Hold the roof in place while you look inside to see if there are any gaps between the roof and the house. Fill them with icing. Hold the roof in place until it stays by itself.

4. Turn the house around so you are looking at the other side.

5. Again, pipe a generous amount of icing down the edges of the two peaks and across the top edge of the remaining side of the house. Also run a line of icing across the edge of the roof that is already attached (see dotted brown lines, below).

6. Press the second roof piece into the icing. Check as well as you can for gaps. Fill any you find. Wait 15–20 minutes before decorating.

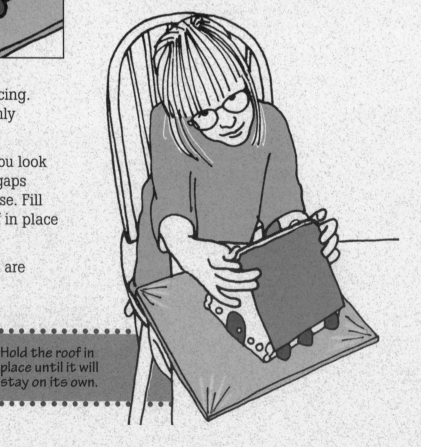

Hold the roof in place until it will stay on its own.

Step 17: Decorating The Roof

Gingerbread Roof

Some gingerbread pieces look too nice to frost! You might consider adding just some finishing touches.

Star Edges: Using a pastry bag with a star tip, squeeze stars along each edge of the roof.

Sugar Snow: Using a sifter, sift confectioners sugar over the gingerbread roof.

Partial Snow: With a knife, spread some white frosting over part of the roof.

Candy Ridge: With a pastry bag or knife, apply a line of icing along the ridge (that's where the two roof pieces meet). Attach gumdrops, mini-marshmallows, or other candy.

Icicles: Use a pastry bag with a medium round tip and white icing. Hold the tip up under the edge of the roof. Squeeze the bag and pull down.

SUCCESS TIPS:

Frost and decorate one side of the roof at a time.

Do not load a lot of heavy candy on the roof. It may collapse!

Frosted Roof

Using a knife, spread icing over the roof. Decorate in any number of ways, including:

Glitter/Sprinkles: Sprinkle with edible glitter, cookie crumbs, shredded coconut, or candy sprinkles. Do it immediately or they will roll off the hardened frosting.

Candy: Attach your favorite candies to the roof randomly or in a pattern.

Frosted Patterns

Using a pastry bag with a small round tip, pipe lines of frosting to form a pattern on either a plain gingerbread or a frosted roof.

Thatched Roof

Pull apart shredded wheat cereal. Frost one side of the roof. Press cereal gently into frosting. Repeat on the other side.

You can make a very simple chimney by attaching a chewy chocolate candy roll to the peak of the roof with frosting. Square candies, bubble gum, root beer barrels, and pretzel nuggets also make good chimneys.

Shingled Roof

Shingles can be made out of gum, cereal, sliced almonds, or crackers. If you use flat sticks of gum, cut each stick into thirds before you attach it to the roof.

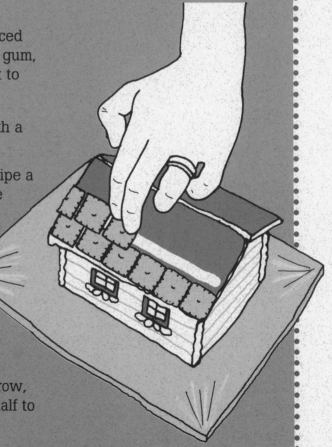

1. To shingle the roof, use a pastry tube with a medium round tip.

2. Starting at the bottom edge of the roof, pipe a line of frosting across the roof. Attach the shingles in a straight row, hanging them over the edge of the roof a little bit.

3. Pipe a line of frosting for the second row. Cut one shingle in half the long way. Attach it above, but overlapping, the first row. Finish the second row, the same as the first.

4. Work your way up the roof. Every other row, you will need to cut the first shingle in half to keep the pattern going.

36

Step 18: Holiday Decorations

Are you building your house around the December holidays? Here are some ideas to make it look festive.

Holly

You will need:

* wax paper
* pastry tube with green icing and leaf tip
* toothpicks
* dab of red icing

1. Spread wax paper on table. Hold the pastry tube at a 45 degree angle to the paper. Squeeze the tube gently and pull it back. A leaf should form.

2. Make a second leaf so that the fat sides touch.

3. With the toothpick, place three dabs of red frosting (berries) where the leaves meet. Allow holly to harden overnight.

4. Gently peel holly off wax paper. Attach to the house with icing. Holly looks great on windows, doors, even roofs.

Candles

You will need:

* snips of red string licorice
* toothpicks
* dab of yellow or orange icing

1. Using a knife or pastry bag, put a dot of frosting on the windowsill. It can be the color of the window trim, or white to look like snow.

2. Press one end of licorice into frosting with the candle standing up on the sill.

3. With a toothpick, dab a little yellow or orange icing onto the top of the licorice for the flame. Candles look great alone, together in a group to form a menorah, or decorated with holly.

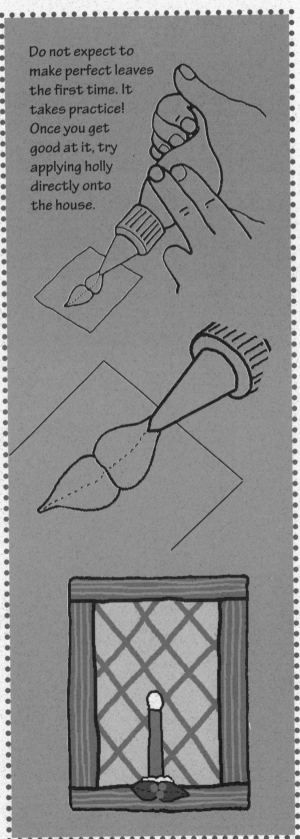

Do not expect to make perfect leaves the first time. It takes practice! Once you get good at it, try applying holly directly onto the house.

37

Wreaths

You will need:

* green gumdrop circles
* pastry bag with red icing and a small round tip

1. Lay a gumdrop circle on the table. To make a bow, squeeze two circles of red icing onto the gumdrop circle. (It should look like a sideways figure eight.) Squeeze two short lines of icing coming from the center of the eight to make the bow ends.

2. Let the bow harden before attaching the wreath to the house with icing. Wreaths look great on walls, doors, or under windows.

Holiday Lights

Many candies work well as holiday lights. Line the edges of the roof, doors and windows with candy buttons, or small candy confetti. You can also use multicolored dots of icing along a "wire" of string licorice!

A variety of wreaths can be made by placing small gumdrops, jelly beans, or frosting stars in a circle. Or use a large star tip and make a ridged circle of frosting. Place the bow to cover where the ends overlap.

Step 19: The Yard

Once your house is completely decorated, it's time to work on your yard.
While your house is hardening, you can make bushes, trees, or snowpeople.

Bushes

You will need:

* wax paper
* kitchen knife
* marshmallows
* green icing
* decorations (colored sugar, sprinkles, coconut, or edible glitter)

1. Using the knife, cover marshmallows with green icing.

2. Sprinkle with colored sugar, coconut, etc.

3. Harden overnight on wax paper.

Trees

You will need:

* wax paper
* kitchen knife
* pointy ice cream cones
* icing (green or white)
* decorations (colored sugar, sprinkles, coconut, edible glitter, or small candies)

1. Place a cone over your second and third fingers. Spread icing onto the cone with the knife.

2. Roll the cone in colored sugar, coconut, sprinkles, or edible glitter – or decorate with candies.

3. Harden overnight on wax paper.

 SUCCESS TIPS:

Candy spearmint leaves make great ready-made bushes. Attach to the walls of your house with icing.

You can dye shredded coconut green by shaking it in a small plastic bag with a few drops of liquid food coloring.

Trees can be plain or fancy.

Snowpeople

For each snowperson, you will need:

* wax paper
* kitchen knife
* 2 marshmallows
* white icing
* 2 pretzel sticks
* small candies
* licorice snip

1. Spread wax paper out on the table. With the kitchen knife, spread a small amount of icing on the top of one marshmallow. Stick the second marshmallow to the first one.

2. Lay snowperson on the wax paper. Push pretzel sticks into the bottom marshmallow (one on each side) to make arms.

3. Using icing, attach a face made of small candies and a licorice snip. Add buttons, too.

4. Using icing, attach a small candy to the head for a hat.

5. Harden overnight.

standard snowperson

chocolate wafer cookie

chocolate candy roll

cowboy

Mr. Fancy Hat

tip of ice cream cone

shredded wheat

gnome or jester

lady

You can make snow-people to match the style of your house. For example, a jester goes well with the castle.

Step 20: Putting It All Together

Your house is decorated. You have made items for your yard. The last step is to put it all together!

To finish off your yard, you will need:

* batch of white or green icing (snow vs. grass)
* small pieces of chocolate, cookies, or caramels
* kitchen knife
* confectioners sugar
* sifter

> Make sure <u>everything</u> is hardened before you try to move the house – wait at least 12 hours!

1. Carefully slide a knife under each side of your house. This should separate the house from the plastic. Gently move the house aside. Remove the plastic wrap from the cardboard. Throw the plastic away, but you will reuse the cardboard.

2. With the knife, spread icing on the area where you will be placing the house. Carefully move your house onto the icing.

3. Frost the area just in front of the door. Use small pieces of chocolate, cookies, or caramels to build front steps. Dabs of icing will hold them in place.

Paths

How about a path leading to your house? Here are a few ideas:

* Dirt paths – use crumbled gingerbread or chocolate cookies.
* Stepping stones – use candy pieces, wads of gum, or walnut halves.
* Brick walks – use small rectangular candies or gum.
* Slate walks – use broken pieces of flat candy or broken gingerbread pieces.

Frost only the area where the path will go. Press your path material into the frosting.

> DON'T PANIC! Once your house is completely hardened, you <u>can</u> move it!

After the path is done, it's time to attach your bushes, trees, and snowpeople. Decide where you'll place them <u>before</u> you frost the yard.

1. Frost the rest of the yard.

2. Place the bushes, trees, and snowpeople where you want them. If you change your mind, move them sooner rather than later so they don't harden in place.

3. As a final touch, sift confectioners sugar over the house and yard so it looks like it has been snowing.

SUCCESS TIP:
Do not put trees or other items too close to the house. You want everyone to see all your hard work!

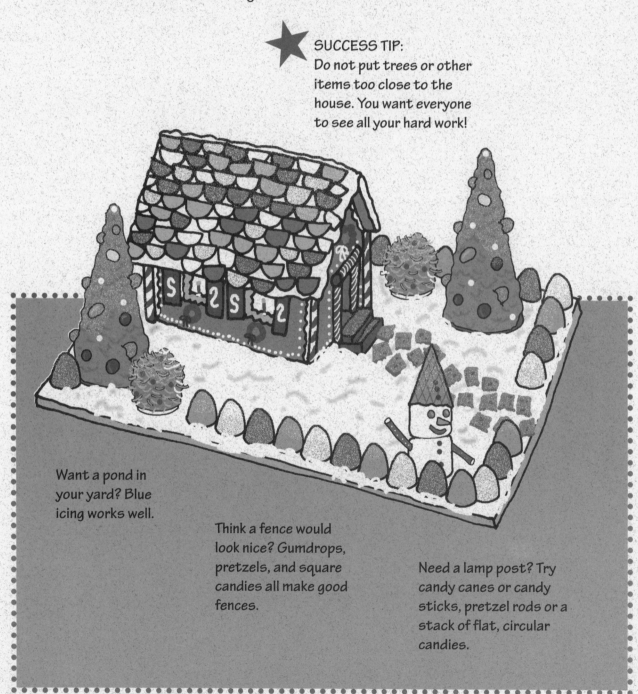

Want a pond in your yard? Blue icing works well.

Think a fence would look nice? Gumdrops, pretzels, and square candies all make good fences.

Need a lamp post? Try candy canes or candy sticks, pretzel rods or a stack of flat, circular candies.

No More Steps: All Done!

Now that your house is finished, you'll have to decide what to do with it. Will you eat it or leave it on display? Will you keep it for yourself, or give it away? Whatever you decide, <u>take a picture of your house</u>!

Gingerbread houses are not permanent. Enjoy them while they last and have the photographs to drool over for years to come.

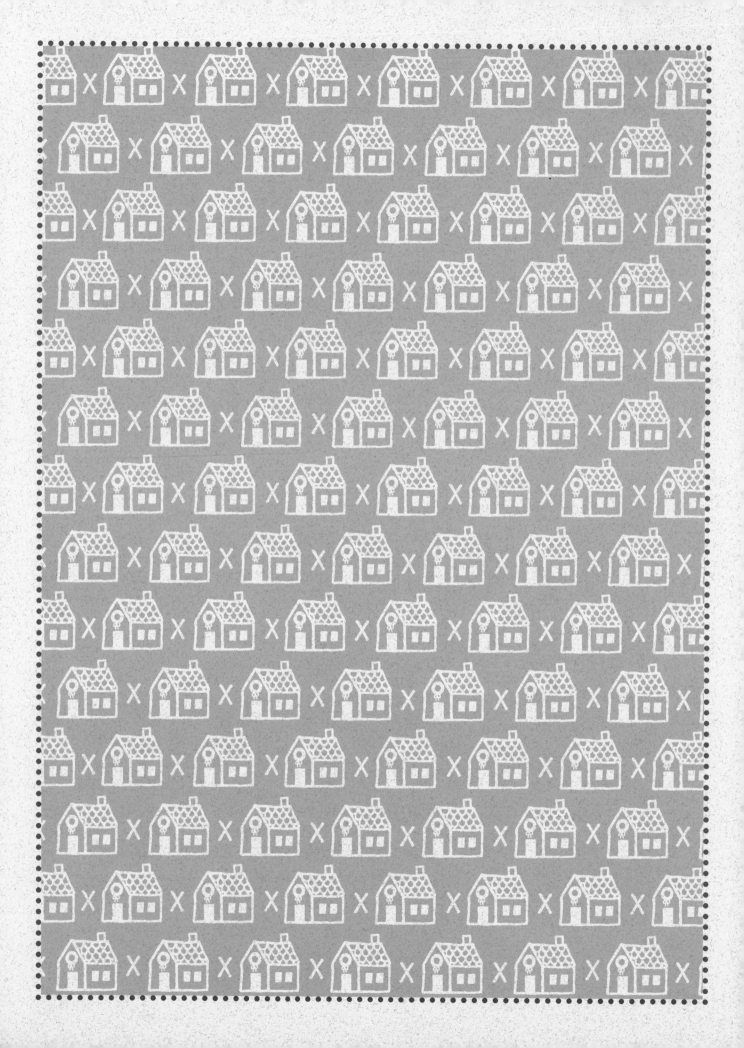

Part II: Other Patterns & Building Instructions

"These houses are the BEST!"

"They are sooooo tasty!"

"And easy to make, too!"

Five More Patterns To Try

If making one gingerbread house has you itching to build another one, here are five more patterns to try – a Chalet, a Church, a Barn, a School, and a Castle. Each structure is built using the same basic steps you've already learned.

✱ The Chalet and the Church are as easy as the Cottage.

✱ The Barn has a different type of roof, but is not difficult.

✱ The School and the Castle can be a little tricky, but are well worth it.

Who knows – you could end up making an entire village!

Church

Castle

Chalet

School

Barn

Chalet

Additional Materials: None

Special Instructions: None

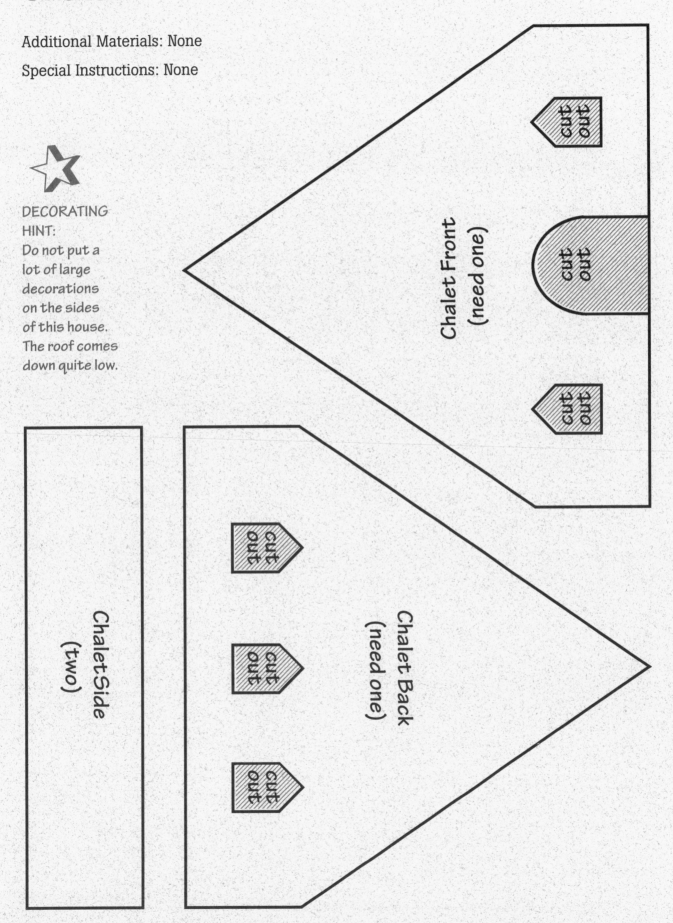

DECORATING
HINT:
Do not put a
lot of large
decorations
on the sides
of this house.
The roof comes
down quite low.

Chalet Front
(need one)

cut out

cut out

cut out

ChaletSide
(two)

Chalet Back
(need one)

cut out

cut out

cut out

DECORATING HINT:
Cut strips of gum to make skis. Thin pretzel sticks or uncooked spaghetti with a piece of round candy or cereal stuck on the end make great ski poles.

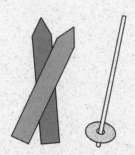

Chalet Roof
(need two)

Church

Additional Materials: one pointy sugar ice cream cone

Special Instructions:

1. The ice cream cone will be the steeple on the church. Ice it as you would a tree (see Step 19). Allow to harden.
2. To attach the steeple, apply a generous amount of icing to the roof near the front peak of the church. Set cone into icing. Allow to harden.

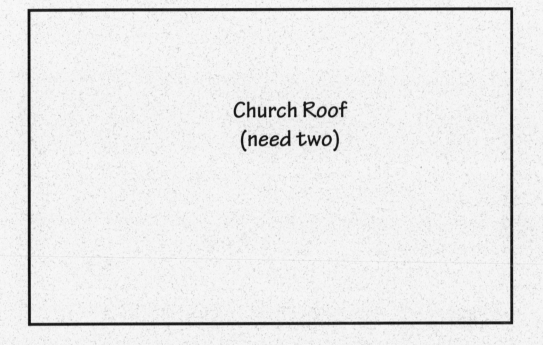

Church Roof
(need two)

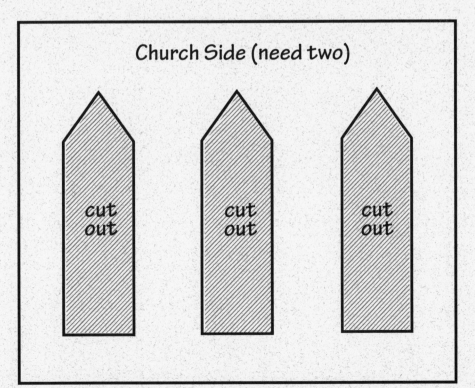

Church Side (need two)

cut out

cut out

cut out

DECORATING HINT: Stained glass windows look great on this pattern! An easy way to make them is to frost each window and stick snips of pastel mini-marshmallows or broken pieces of hard candy into the icing. Do one window at a time so the icing doesn't harden before you have a chance to stick in the window pieces.

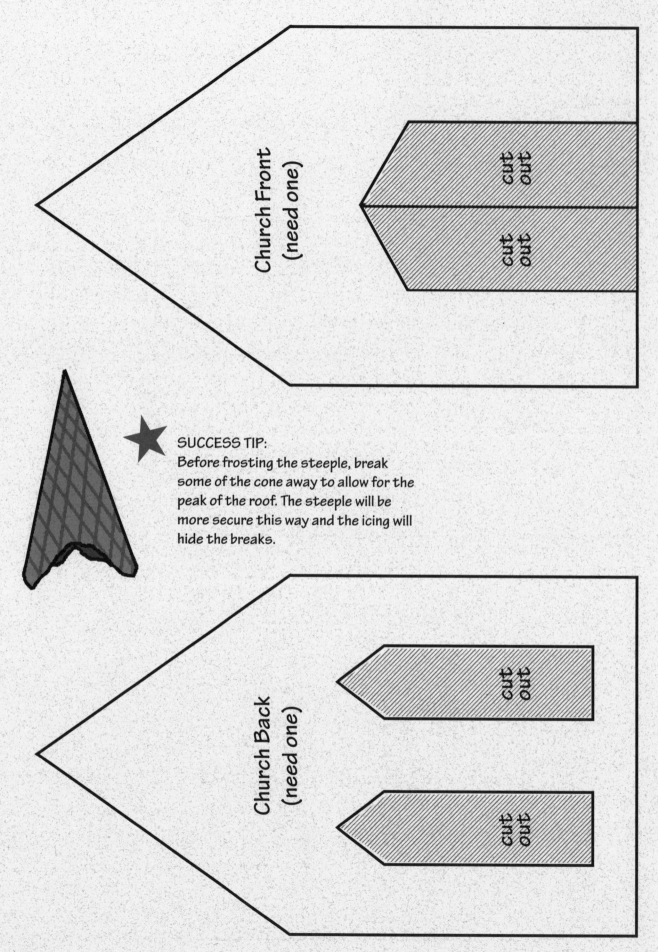

Church Front
(need one)

cut out

cut out

SUCCESS TIP:
Before frosting the steeple, break
some of the cone away to allow for the
peak of the roof. The steeple will be
more secure this way and the icing will
hide the breaks.

Church Back
(need one)

cut out

cut out

Barn

Additional Materials: None

Special Instructions: The Barn is the only building with more than two roof pieces. The upper pieces should be attached first, then the lower ones.

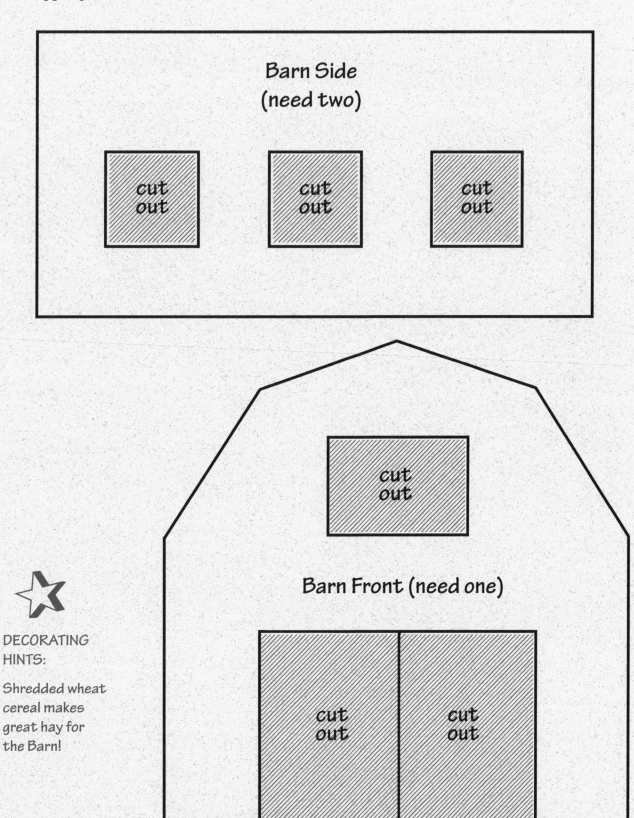

DECORATING HINTS:

Shredded wheat cereal makes great hay for the Barn!

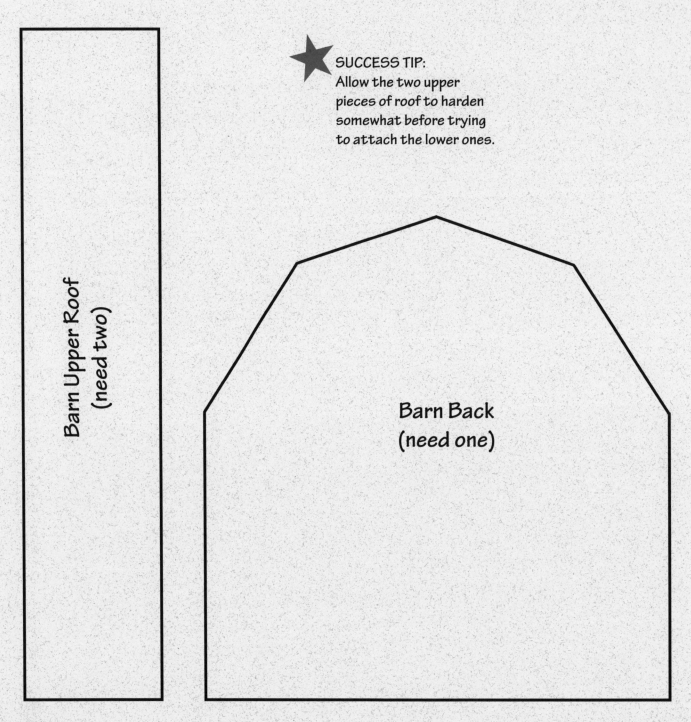

Barn Lower Roof
(need two)

SUCCESS TIP:
Allow the two upper
pieces of roof to harden
somewhat before trying
to attach the lower ones.

Barn Upper Roof
(need two)

Barn Back
(need one)

School (with bell tower)

Additional Materials: one gumdrop or other small candy for bell

Special Instructions: Follow the basic steps for the main part of the School. The bell tower is assembled separately. The tower consists of four roof pieces, four window pieces, and a small square base. Make sure you have all nine pieces before trying to put the tower together.

The bell tower is assembled in several stages:

1. Lay the four windows around the small gingerbread square. The windows that go over the roof peaks should be on opposite sides. To be sure they are lined up correctly, pretend you can stand in the middle of the gingerbread square. Can you see the letter "M" formed by each window as you turn around? (see diagram)

2. Pipe icing around the top edges of the base. Assemble the windows on top of the base, as you would the sides of a house. Allow to harden.

3. Pipe a large dot of icing into the center of the square. Press a small gumdrop or other candy into this dot to make the bell. Allow to harden for 15-20 minutes.

4. Turn the structure over. Pipe icing around the top edges of the square.

5. Pipe icing down one edge of a roof piece from the point to the base. Take that piece and another roof piece. Press both pieces into the icing on the base and gently lean toward the center until they meet.

6. Repeat this process until all four pieces are attached. Allow to harden another 15-20 minutes.

7. To attach the bell tower to the School, pipe icing along the bottom edges and gently place the V-edges over the peak of the roof near the front of the School. Allow to harden.

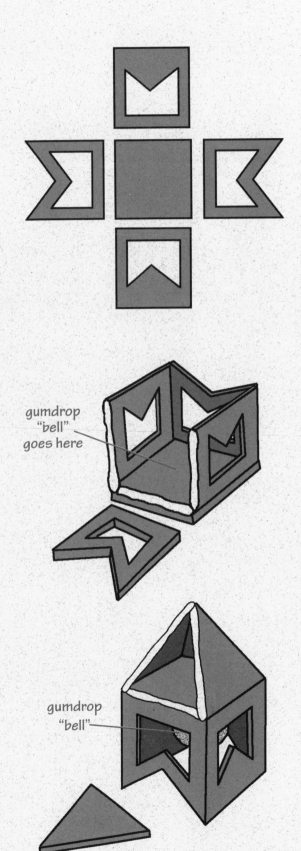

gumdrop "bell" goes here

gumdrop "bell"

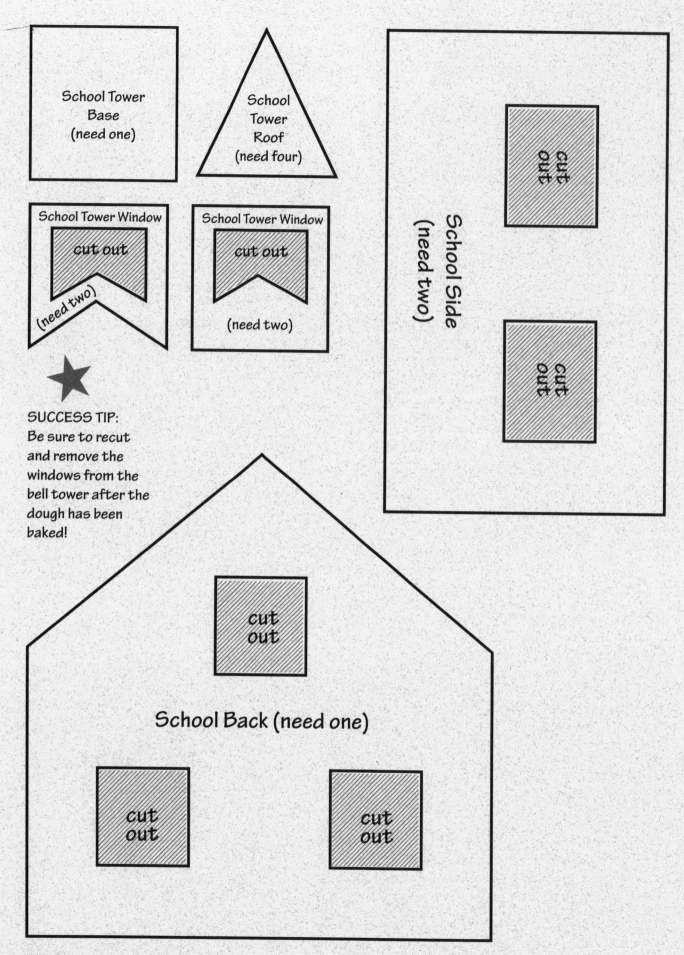

School Tower Base (need one)

School Tower Roof (need four)

School Tower Window

cut out

(need two)

School Tower Window

cut out

(need two)

SUCCESS TIP: Be sure to recut and remove the windows from the bell tower after the dough has been baked!

School Side (need two)

cut out

cut out

cut out

School Back (need one)

cut out

cut out

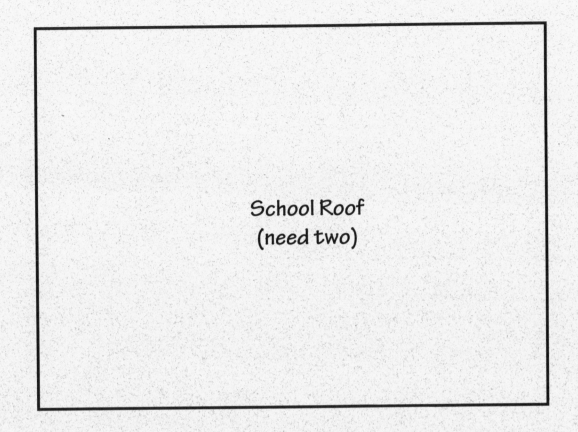

School Roof
(need two)

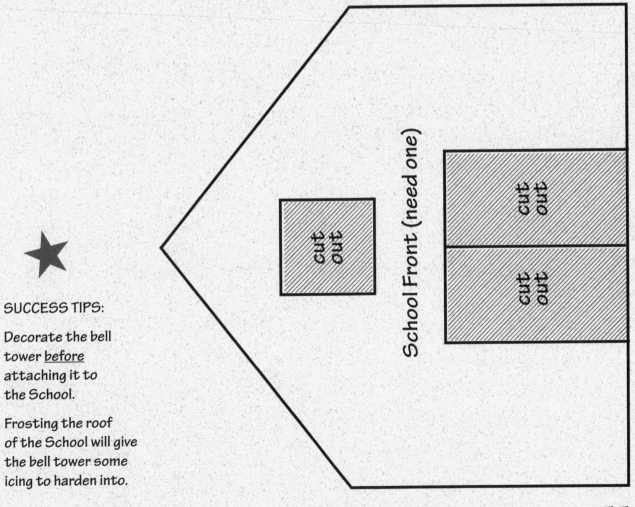

School Front (need one)

cut
out

cut
out

cut
out

SUCCESS TIPS:

Decorate the bell tower _before_ attaching it to the School.

Frosting the roof of the School will give the bell tower some icing to harden into.

Castle

Additional Materials:

* four wafer ice cream cones with flat bottoms
* small gumdrops and licorice string (optional)

Special Instructions: The Castle does NOT follow the same steps as the Cottage. The Castle is the only building with a base. It is also the only building without a roof.

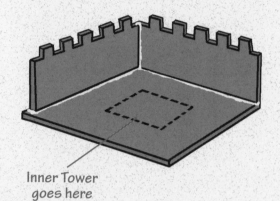

Inner Tower goes here

The Outer Walls

The outer walls of the Castle are put together like the sides of a house – but on top of the base. Be sure to pipe icing on the edges of the base when you put the walls on top of it.

Inner Tower

The inner tower should be built and decorated separately from the outer walls. After it's all done and hardened, pipe icing along the bottom edges and place carefully inside the outer walls. It should sit in the center of the base.

Outer Towers

The four ice cream cones are the outer towers. Apply icing with a knife or a pastry tube to the bottom of the cone. Set firmly into each corner of the outer walls.

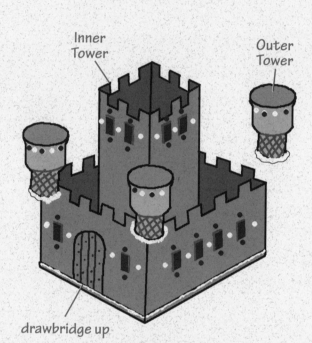

Inner Tower

Outer Tower

drawbridge up

Drawbridge

If you want the drawbridge UP on your Castle, trace it as you would a door or window, but don't remove the door piece. If you want the drawbridge DOWN, be sure to cut out the door and remove it after the wall is baked. Save the door to use as the drawbridge. Attach the drawbridge after the Castle is completely decorated.

Moat

Blue icing makes terrific water for a moat. Lay the drawbridge over the moat.

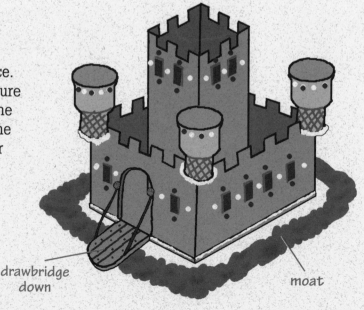

drawbridge down

moat

SUCCESS TIPS:

Attach the inner tower <u>before</u> putting on the outer towers.

If you wish to ice and/ or decorate the outer towers, it's easier to do it <u>before</u> attaching them. Allow to harden before setting them in place.

DECORATING HINTS:

Small rectangular sticks of gum make perfect windows on the Castle.

Wafer cones (for the outer towers) are available in colors like pink, green, and brown.

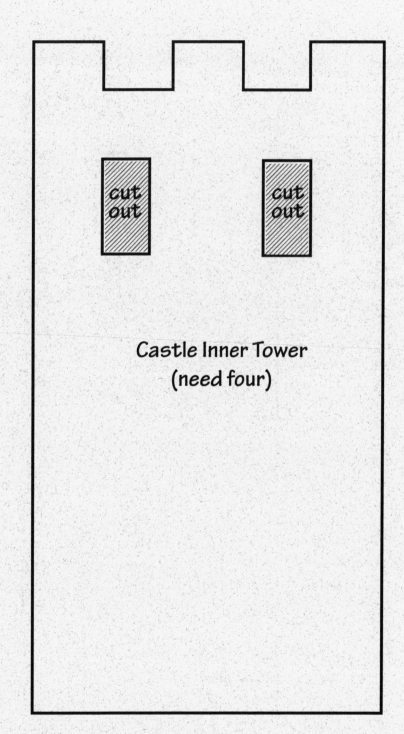

Castle Inner Tower
(need four)

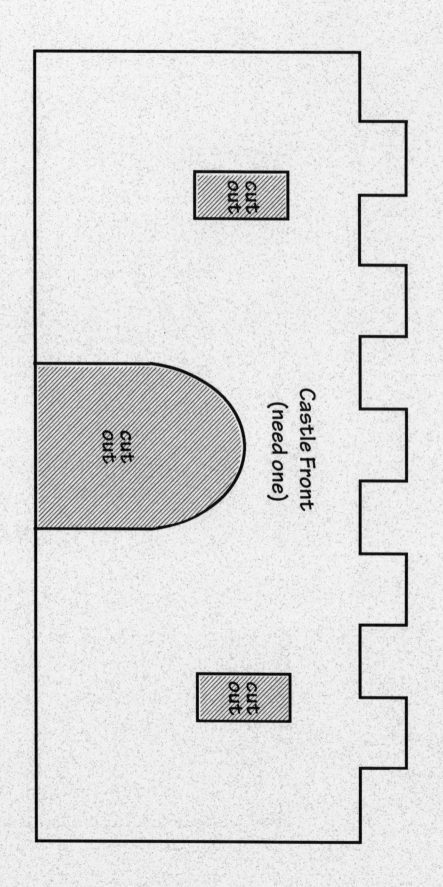

Castle Front
(need one)

cut
out

cut
out

cut
out

58

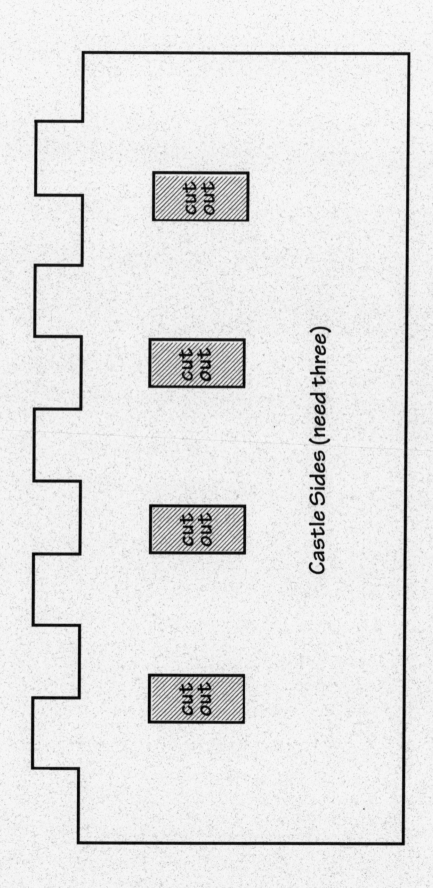

Castle Sides (need three)

Castle Base
8-1/2 x 8-1/2 inches
(need one)

After photocopying this page, merely
cut on this line to get the base pattern.

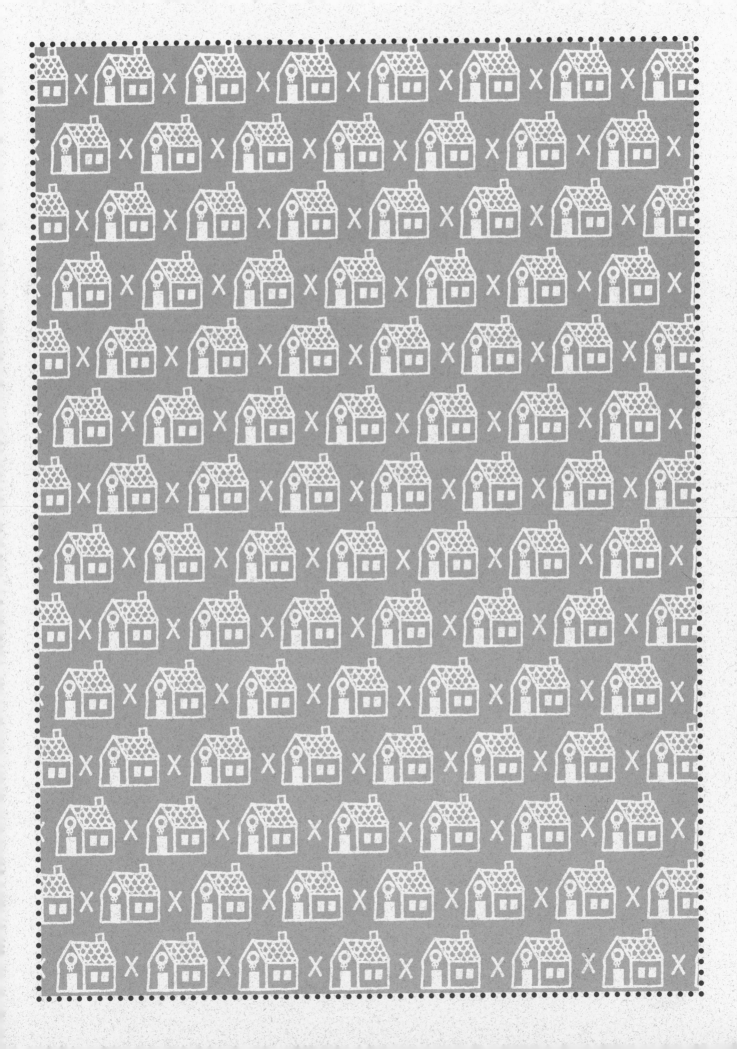

Checklist Of Tools & Equipment

- [ ] stove/oven
- [ ] large pot (8 quart)
- [ ] wooden spoon
- [ ] 1 cup measuring cup
- [ ] measuring spoons (teaspoon, tablespoon)
- [ ] cookie sheet(s) (the type with one or two raised edges preferred)
- [ ] rolling pin
- [ ] small sharp knife
- [ ] photocopy of pattern
- [ ] scissors
- [ ] oven mitts
- [ ] cooling rack(s)
- [ ] pancake turner
- [ ] wastebasket
- [ ] file
- [ ] sturdy piece of cardboard, wood, or plastic (for base)

- [ ] plastic wrap
- [ ] tape
- [ ] electric mixer
- [ ] mixing bowl
- [ ] pastry bag(s)
- [ ] coupler(s)
- [ ] decorating tips (round, star, leaf and shutter)
- [ ] zigzag cake decorating tool (optional)
- [ ] paste food coloring
- [ ] spoons
- [ ] small airtight containers
- [ ] small paintbrush
- [ ] bent-handled knife
- [ ] wax paper
- [ ] toothpicks
- [ ] paper towels
- [ ] no-stick cooking spray

Checklist Of Building Materials

Dough

- ☐ butter
- ☐ sugar
- ☐ unsulphured molasses
- ☐ flour
- ☐ baking soda
- ☐ nutmeg
- ☐ salt
- ☐ ginger

Icing

- ☐ confectioners sugar
- ☐ meringue powder
- ☐ cream of tartar
- ☐ water

Decorations

- ☐ your choice of candies, crackers, nuts, etc. for decorating the house
- ☐ ice cream cones, marshmallows, pretzel sticks, etc. for building yard items (optional)

Church

- ☐ one pointy sugar ice cream cone (for steeple)

School

- ☐ gumdrop or other small candy (for bell)

Castle

- ☐ four wafer ice cream cones with flat bottoms (for towers)
- ☐ small gumdrops and licorice string (for drawbridge) (optional)

Order Form

	Qty.	Subtotal
Gingerbread Houses For Kids .... $14.95 each		
<u>Shipping & Handling</u> *$3.00 for one book* *.50 for each additional book*	Shipping & Handling:	
	Total Enclosed:	

Please make checks or money orders payable in U.S. dollars to:

White Birch Press, P.O. Box 1433, Concord, NH 03302-1433

Ship To: _____

Address: _____

_____

Daytime Phone: _____

• •

Order Form

	Qty.	Subtotal
Gingerbread Houses For Kids .... $14.95 each		
<u>Shipping & Handling</u> *$3.00 for one book* *.50 for each additional book*	Shipping & Handling:	
	Total Enclosed:	

Please make checks or money orders payable in U.S. dollars to:

White Birch Press, P.O. Box 1433, Concord, NH 03302-1433

Ship To: _____

Address: _____

_____

Daytime Phone: _____